VIRTUE STORIES

Handle with Care

Lalita Iyer

Om KIDZ
An imprint of Om Books International

Ali couldn't wait any more! His mum was on her way home with his baby brother.

Ali had met his brother a few days ago. He hadn't been able to visit him again although he badly wanted to. The doctors had given strict instructions that he shouldn't go to the hospital because of his cold. Ali wasn't too upset as he knew all about germs and what they could do, especially to a small baby.

Besides, his baby brother was the bringer of many gifts - a shining red toy truck, a set of dinosaurs and his favourite - a big drum that someone had gifted and Papa kept away on the highest shelf in his room. 'The neighbours will get disturbed,' Papa said by way of explaining, when Ali insisted on using it during nap time, in the afternoon.

Ali knew that it would take a while for the baby to grow up and until then, the gifts were his. He could not wait for his brother to arrive so that he could show him how everything works!

Just then, the
doorbell rang.
It was Mama
with the baby!

Ali ran straight into his Mama's arms. His brother seemed scared of all the noise and began to cry. Mama put him to bed, though not before Ali gave him a tight squeeze, which made him cry louder.

The next day, Ali introduced his best friend Big Mac, the barking dog, to his brother. Big Mac had a soft bark and Ali brought him close to his brother's ear so he could hear him well. But his brother burst out crying and had to be hurriedly carried away again.

Ali tried to cuddle his brother that night - he was looking adorable in his soft rabbit suit. But his grandma lifted his brother out of reach and only let him look at him. That night, Ali was very sad. When Mama asked him what the matter was, he said that his brother did not like him and always cried when he came near.

Mama said 'hmmm' and looked thoughtful. 'I think it's because he cannot talk and may be, he thinks that you - because you're **So** big and strong compared to how little and weak he is - could hurt him. So maybe, if we could put up a sign that reminded you of how he felt, you would be more gentle with him?'

'Ok, Mama,' Ali said, his eyes shining brightly. 'But what should we put on the sign?'

Mama thought again. 'A "Handle with care" sign would be perfect!' Ali and Mama tore out some sheets of paper from his scrapbook and Mama drew a big skull and Ali put in a big 'X' all over each sheet. Mama said skulls and Xs were signs to tell us to be careful, though she gave the skull a nice big smiley face!

HANDLE WITH CARE
HANDLE WITH CARE
HANDLE WITH CARE
HANDLE WITH CARE

Then they snuck into his brother's nursery. They put the signs up everywhere with a little bit of sticky tape as a reminder for Ali that he would need to be sensitive to his little brother's needs, even though he didn't have the same needs as the little one. The solution worked wonderfully! In a few days, Ali's brother stopped crying. Ali was around him, and they both started their adventures as brothers and best friends.

VIRTUE STORIES

Help is on the Way

Lalita Iyer

Om KIDZ
An imprint of Om Books International

Andre's mouth watered at the juicy mangoes hanging from the tree. It would be a matter of minutes to climb up, pluck a few of the choicest ones and then scamper down again.

He'd sprained his ankle playing football last week and the doctor had told him that he was not to play football for two weeks. *But he hadn't said anything about climbing trees*, Andre thought to himself.

The mango tree was his big secret.

It stood right at the end of a path with a dead end which no one frequented. The mystery lane was lined on both sides with the back walls of huge apartment complexes in which his friends lived.

He planned the route carefully - he'd need to climb just three of the branches to get to the mango that he had his eye on - a large, shiny, glossy orange-yellow one that hung so close, yet so far!

He swung himself higher and higher; and before he knew it, he had plucked his prize off its stem and sunk his teeth into it. Ah! The sweetness and juiciness of a mango fresh off the tree filled his mouth. He propped himself up against the slim bark and took his time enjoying it.

Andre was about to swing back down when he spotted an even larger, bigger prize a few branches up. His ankle had begun to feel a little sore and he knew it was best that he headed back home; but the sweetness of the mango filled his mouth and he swung himself up, up and away!

He was rewarded with not one but three gifts of goodness and at last, his tummy filled with the bliss of mangoes, he decided to descend. But a cool, strong breeze had begun to blow and every time he tried to find a footing on the thin branches below him, the branch swung away and his ankle began to pain a little bit more.

He tried again and again. But it was no good and his ankle now throbbed with a fierce pain.

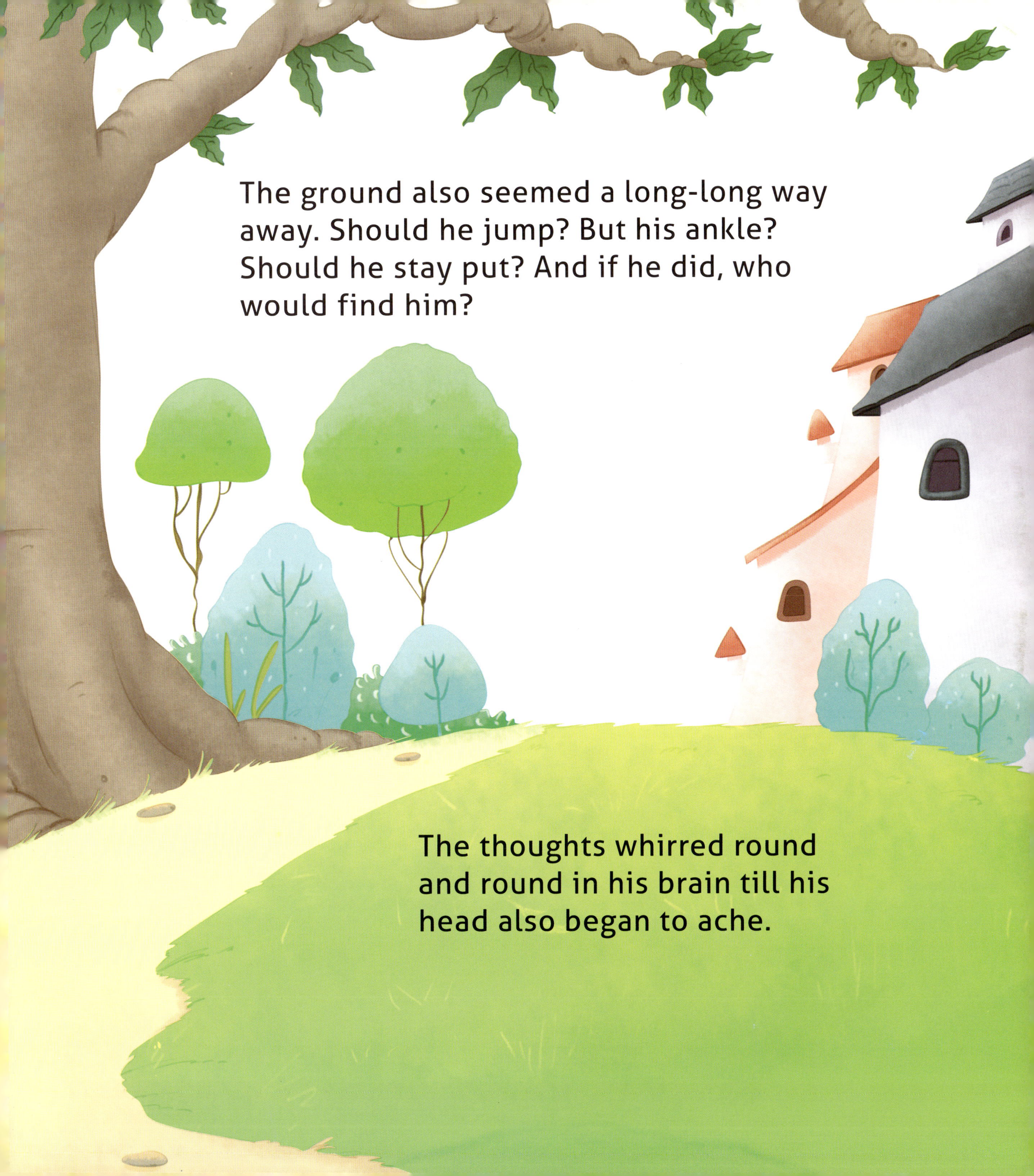

The ground also seemed a long-long way away. Should he jump? But his ankle? Should he stay put? And if he did, who would find him?

The thoughts whirred round and round in his brain till his head also began to ache.

Andre took one last look at the ground, sat back against the trunk and decided to wait. He knew his father would come for him if he was absent another half hour, he told himself. Yes! His father would definitely come. He had to believe. *Didn't Daddy always say he would look out for him?*

Though the tears began to trickle out of his eyes, he stayed put. He hoped and tried to think positively.

After what seemed like hours of waiting since he had left home (though it couldn't have been hours as the sun had not set yet), he heard someone calling out to him. 'Annnnddreeeeeeeee!'

It was Daddy!

Andre hollered as loud as he could: 'I'm here Daddy, right here. Come soon! I'm waiting.'

He knew he was safe now.

VIRTUE STORIES

Oh that's Rude

Lalita Iyer

An imprint of Om Books International

When the snack break bell rang, the Year 2 children rushed out of the class. Snack or not, they never missed playing on the field. Especially since Ryan joined their class.

Ryan came up with the most interesting games to spend time: seven tiles, land and water, superpower games, catching cook, four corners, chain tag and much more.

Yes, Ryan had the best ideas but he was mostly angry or grumpy and never smiled easily. He had to be pleaded with to play with them. When someone didn't understand the rules of his game, he was quick to get angry and said some very rude things like "Oh, you are so dumb!" or something like that.

The last time, he told Megan, "I think you should just sit in a corner and watch. You are too slow for this game." She was so upset, she burst into tears.

Yet, all the kids in the group wanted to be part of his cool games. They usually ignored his rudeness because playing with him was so much fun.

One day, Tomas from Spain joined their class. He was not very familiar with English, but he was very friendly and extremely polite. When he joined the group for their snack break game, he too was quite excited about playing the games that Ryan knew.

Now there were two problems; he did not understand the rules too well and he didn't know English too well. So he kept making mistakes, slowing down the game.

As usual, Ryan lost his temper and shouted at Tomas, "First learn English and then come and play with us!" Poor Tomas walked away with tears rolling down his cheeks. Luckily, he found another group of children to play board games with.

Now, the other eight children in Ryan's group really, really liked Tomas, and soon started missing him. Ryan was also beginning to get more and more annoying. They decided to spend snack time playing board games with Tomas. And guess what? Tomas could make his own board games!

After a week, Ryan was left with nobody to play with. Everyone was now Team Tomas.

Ryan felt awfully lonely. He saw how his old group was having a great time with Tomas at the board games table.

That night he felt very upset with himself. He realised his rudeness had chased people out of his group. *But what could he do now? Was it too late? There must be a way,* he thought.

He finally had a plan.

Ryan walked into the school the next morning, and the first thing that he did was to find Tomas and the group of eight children. "Hi guys," he said, walking up to them. "I am really sorry. I have been so badly behaved these past few months. But it won't happen again. Promise."

The group looked at each other. No one spoke. They didn't know if Ryan actually meant what he was saying. And then Tomas spoke.

"It's okay. It happens. By the way, do you want to play Risk? I just learnt it. We could play at break time. "

After a couple of hours, when the snack break bell rang, you could see Ryan and Tomas and the entire gang discussing new game ideas and rules with an excited group on the field.

Ryan was never lonely, never rude and never without a smile ever again.

VIRTUE STORIES

When in doubt, tell the Truth

Lalita Iyer

Om KIDZ
An imprint of Om Books International

Matt came home from school, threw his satchel, gulped his smoothie and was ready to dash off to play.

'You seem really eager to go out and play these days,' said his mom.

She was right. Matt had made a new friend Joe, in the apartment block. The fact was that more than playing football with him, which they did, Matt loved listening to Joe's stories about the XBox games he played at home. Joe was eleven, four years older than Matt and Matt loved that an older, much taller boy enjoyed playing with him. It made him feel very special.

That day, after kicking around a bit, Joe casually asked, 'Want to come to my place and play a shooting game? There is no one at home.'

Matt knew that he wasn't allowed.

'But... but... my mom says...'

'There's no need to tell your mom. No one will know. Come for a bit?'

Tempted, Matt went along. He knew mom would be furious if she came to know. He wasn't allowed to play video games or to go to anyone's house without her permission. He went, anyway.

When they reached the house, he was secretly happy Joe's mother was not at home. 'Let's do double player,' he said, handing Joe a controller and encouraged him. 'Go for it!'

There was a lot of shooting in the game but Matt kept shooting the wrong guys and Joe kept getting annoyed at him. Finally he said, 'Okay, may be you just sit there and watch me,' taking back the controller from Matt.

For the next hour, Joe also stopped talking to him and soon, Matt had a headache because of the noisy gunfire, but he said nothing. He felt like crying but what could he do?

After a brief silence, he quietly got up and went home and began to do his homework. Joe barely said bye to him when he left.

When his mother entered his room, she was surprised. 'You are here? I thought I'll pick you up from the football ground, but I couldn't find you.'

'Oh...I ...I...'Matt muttered uncomfortably, wondering what to say.

'You decided to come home early and do your homework and please your mamma?' she said. 'What a good boy you are!'

Matt was confused. His mom trusted him so much! He could have easily got away with it this time. But something bothered him inside about hiding stuff from her.

'Actually mamma, I did something you won't approve.'

'Really? What?'

'Well, I went to play X box at Joe's house, but I didn't like it, so I came home.' Matt's mother was really shaken.

She wondered. *Is he in bad company? Should I be worried? What if he ends up playing some violent games? How dangerous is this?* A thousand thoughts rushed through her mind. But she decided to stay calm.

Matt, after all, had spoken the truth when he could have easily got away with not telling her.

'I am glad you told me, Matt. I really appreciate your honesty,' she said hugging him tightly.

As she put her things away, she added, 'Maybe I could download some non-shooting games for you on my iPad and you could play for half-an-hour every day after homework. How does that sound?

Matt couldn't believe his ears! So, speaking the truth had some rewards after all!

VIRTUE STORIES

Do it Yourself

Lalita Iyer

Om KIDZ
An imprint of Om Books International

'Please fasten your seatbelts.' The pilot said, 'The plane will be landing shortly.'

Nadine was very excited. It was the first time she was visiting New York. She had been looking forward to meeting her aunt and cousins all summer!

On reaching their aunt's house, her two cousins - Dan and Sam, raced to the car even before they had barely stepped out of it.

Everyone went inside, chattering away, looking happy.

Nadine went to her room to freshen up and then went down for dinner. 'Nadine, be a doll and take these plates to the dining room, will you? I don't know where Sam and Dan have disappeared.' Her aunt said, looking absolutely exhausted as she stirred something in a big vessel.

This was very puzzling. You see, Nadine was from Mumbai and like most of the rich people from Mumbai she had house help commonly known as 'servants'.

This meant that Nadine never had to do any work! Everything was taken care of, by the help. She had never ever laid a table in her life!

However, in America, most people couldn't afford house help. They did everything all by themselves!

Nadine took the plates, anyway; And then she took the spoons and forks; and then the table mats; and then the food. *This laying the table thing was kind of fun.*

When they all sat down for dinner, the table looked different. Nadine couldn't help admiring herself at what a good job she had done. It felt nice to have done something without the help.

This was fun. I wonder why they call it chores, she wondered. She now looked forward to what else she could do to help Aunt Naomi. And there was plenty!

Every day, she would hang out her wet towels to dry, she'd fold her own clothes and make her own bed. After every task she did, she felt a little thrill. She resolved that when she went back home after her holidays in America, she would do the same. The help needed a break too!

Nadine had finally begun doing things by herself and what a joy that was!

VIRTUE STORIES

I am not Scared

Lalita Iyer

Om KIDZ
An imprint of Om Books International

Maya got a big fat zero in the Maths test. Again. She had forgotten to tell Mama about it on Friday; and now Mama had to sign the paper or they would call Mama tomorrow and complain, which in her experience was far worse.

She was so scared! Mama would be angry. She toyed with trying to copy Mama's signature. She had her homework diary.

She must try. How hard could it be? But when she opened it, her heart sank.

The signature was a swirly-curvy set of dancing letters that she could never copy!

She decided to fall sick instead. Maybe they would forget to ask about the paper the day after!

She thought deeply on the bus back about how to fall sick. To her friend's surprise, she turned down a game of who-can-slap-my-hand-the-quickest (at which she was the undisputed champion). At last, she came up with a plan!

She would have a cold water shower. That would bring on a fever immediately. The only thing was that she hated getting wet in cold water. She decided she would just have to do it, as she was scared about what Mama would do if she found out!

As a backup plan, she decided to tuck two onions into her armpits prior to her bath, and hang out in the bathroom for a bit - she'd read it also induced immediate fever. She hated onions and the smell made her want to barf. She would just have to do it as she was scared of the consequences otherwise.

Later that evening, as Mama made dinner, Maya sat shivering in the bathroom.The onions, skin and all - were safely, but very uncomfortably, sitting under her armpits.

Within a few minutes though, her arms and shoulders ached, her armpits began to scratch. She hid the onions in the drawer full of lotions, perfumes and other toiletries and decided to take a longer-than-planned-for-shower.

But the water was cold! Brrr!!

She poked at the water with her finger tips; she'd start getting wet a little bit at a time.

Then she stuck out her toes and withdrew them almost instantly. She tried her arms next; dancing sideways and backwards as the icy droplets fell in merry abandon. This wasn't working either.

Maya dried herself and came out. Mama had called her for dinner at least thrice by now. She was very quiet at dinner. Mama asked her if she was fine and she forgot and said 'yes,' and then it was too late to go back and say 'no,' as Nikki began crying and Mama hurried off to give him his bottle.

' Is everything fine, Maya?' Mama asked her as she tucked her into bed. Maya nodded, but the tears began to roll down her cheeks. 'What is the matter Maya?' Mama asked. Maya plucked up courage and decided, *I will not be chicken. I will just do it.* And she told Mama everything.

To her surprise Mama praised her for telling the truth and promised to sign the paper. Maya agreed to wake up early to redo the sums she'd made mistakes on. This feeling of being free was wonderful! Mama was not angry and Maya was not scared any more!

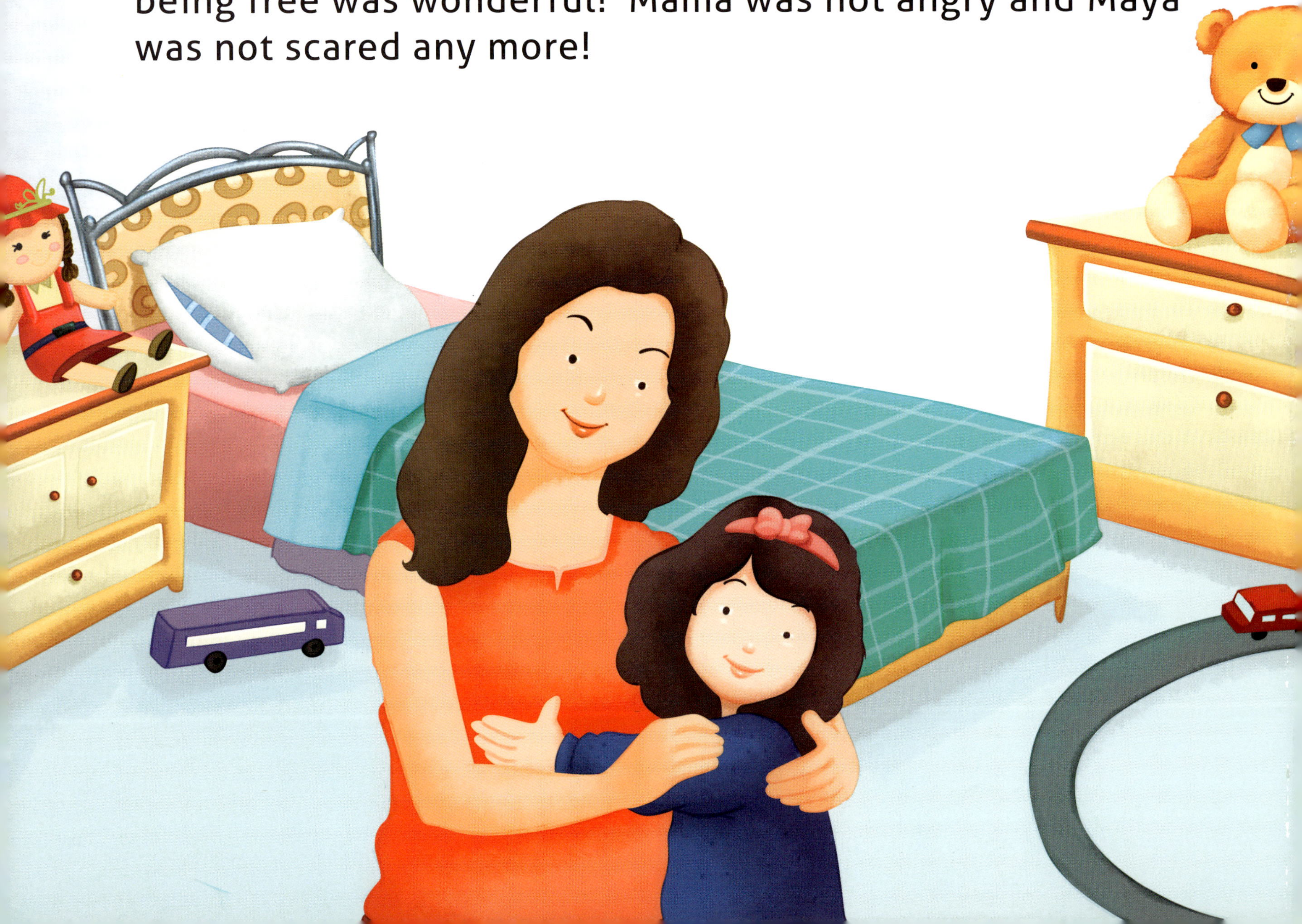